Amazon Parrots Pets

An Amazon Parrot Pet Owner's Guide

Amazon Parrot Facts & Information, where to buy, health, diet, lifespan, types, breeding, fun facts and more!

By: Lolly Brown

Copyrights and Trademarks

All rights reserved. No part of this book may be reproduced or transformed in any form or by any means, graphic, electronic, or mechanical, including photocopying, recording, taping, or by any information storage retrieval system, without the written permission of the author.

This publication is Copyright ©2019 NRB Publishing, an imprint. Nevada. All products, graphics, publications, software and services mentioned and recommended in this publication are protected by trademarks. In such instance, all trademarks & copyright belong to the respective owners. For information consult www.NRBpublishing.com

Disclaimer and Legal Notice

This product is not legal, medical, or accounting advice and should not be interpreted in that manner. You need to do your own due-diligence to determine if the content of this product is right for you. While every attempt has been made to verify the information shared in this publication, neither the author, neither publisher, nor the affiliates assume any responsibility for errors, omissions or contrary interpretation of the subject matter herein. Any perceived slights to any specific person(s) or organization(s) are purely unintentional.

We have no control over the nature, content and availability of the web sites listed in this book. The inclusion of any web site links does not necessarily imply a recommendation or endorse the views expressed within them. We take no responsibility for, and will not be liable for, the websites being temporarily unavailable or being removed from the internet.

The accuracy and completeness of information provided herein and opinions stated herein are not guaranteed or warranted to produce any particular results, and the advice and strategies, contained herein may not be suitable for every individual. Neither the author nor the publisher shall be liable for any loss incurred as a consequence of the use and application, directly or indirectly, of any information presented in this work. This publication is designed to provide information in regard to the subject matter covered.

Neither the author nor the publisher assume any responsibility for any errors or omissions, nor do they represent or warrant that the ideas, information, actions, plans, suggestions contained in this book is in all cases accurate. It is the reader's responsibility to find advice before putting anything written in this book into practice. The information in this book is not intended to serve as legal, medical, or accounting advice.

Foreword

Have you ever wanted a pet bird? You can settle for the cute parakeet or the gentle dove. But why not get a complex and brilliant bird to be your companion? Having an intelligent bird for a pet is surely rewarding. What's more, they are very interactive and you will never have a boring day in your life!

Did you know that behind the charming features of the Amazon parrot is a very big brain and an even bigger tummy? Yes, Amazon parrots are highly intelligent birds that can learn easily, interpret behaviors and communicate with their owners and other people. They are among the largest parrots and love to eat a variety of food. Amazon parrots are typically green with a variety of color—all colors of the rainbow—on their faces and around their necks and head that makes them so captivating.

Keeping an Amazon parrot is not for the faint-hearted. While they can undoubtedly be enjoyable pets as they are quite outgoing and intelligent, they can be a real challenge to have around. You will encounter different behavioral challenges such as biting, excessive chewing, voicing or screaming, hormonal aggression and dominant behaviors. Whether you get a young bird or a rescued one, your pet will need proper guidance and care. You need to have a good understanding of their needs and behaviors as well as know and apply training techniques.

Table of Contents

Introduction 1
Chapter One: The Exotic Amazon Parrot 3
    Why Amazon Parrots are Popular 5
    How Amazon Parrots Communicate 7
    Is the Amazon Parrot the Pet for You? 9
Chapter Two: A Home for Your Amazon Parrot 15
    Different Kinds of Bird Cages 16
    Right Size, Right Design 19
    Proper Placement 20
    Accessories for the Bird Cage 22
        Perches 22
        Bird Toys 23
        Cups 25
        Lighting 26
        Cage Covers 26
        Seed Guards and Bloomers 27
        Play Stand 28
    Cleaning Your Amazon Parrot's Cage 28
    How to Keep Pests Away from the Cage 30
Chapter Three: Amazon Parrot Nutrition 33
    Base Diet + Supplemental Diet 34

Foods to Avoid 36

The Importance of Bird Foraging 39

Chapter Four: Good Grooming for Your Amazon Parrot.... 41

Beak Trimming 42

Wing Clipping 43

Molting 44

Bathing 45

Chapter Five: Training Your Amazon Parrot 51

In the Beginning 51

It's All about Trust 53

Before Taming and Training 54

Taming a New Amazon Parrot 57

Training a Shy Amazon Parrot 58

Taming a Fearful Amazon Parrot 61

Training your Amazon Parrot to Talk 63

Stages of Talking 67

Training your Amazon Parrot to "Step Up" 69

Stick Training Your Amazon Parrot 71

Potty Training your Amazon Parrot 73

Using Positive Reinforcement in Training 74

More Tricks? 75

Chapter Six: Can You Discipline an Amazon Parrot? 77

Dealing with Behavior 81

    Preening 81

    Body Language 83

    Plucking 85

    Being "One - Person Birds" 86

Your Amazon Parrot's Behavior Can Be Affected by Hormones 87

Dealing with Your Amazon Parrot 88

Chapter Seven: Caring for Your Bird's Health and Getting the Right Vet 91

    Respiratory Infections 92

    Viral Diseases 93

    Bacterial Infections 93

    Nutrient Deficiencies 94

    Cancer 96

Cloacal Papillomas 96

Getting the Right Parrot Doctor 97

Common Dangers inside the Home 100

Signs that Your Amazon Parrot May Be Sick or Injured 103

Conclusion 107

    Glossary of Important Terms 111

Photo Credits 117

References 119

Introduction

While they are truly appealing, it is not their looks that make them so popular as pets. This parrot species is most desired because it has the ability to talk. Not every parrot can learn to pick up sounds but the Amazon parrot can mimic sounds, more than other species. And unlike the African grey parrots—also a popular species—that can perfectly imitate a sound, the Amazon parrot normally retains a part of its voice so you can distinguish that it is the parrot speaking and it's not simply an echo. Amazon parrots are also amazing singers as they love music and will be more inclined to imitate music more than other parrots.

Introduction

The gorgeous Blue - Fronted Amazon parrot is one of the most popular Amazon parrots. But there are many different species that are available as companion pets such as the Yellow-Naped Amazons, Red-Lored Amazons, Lilac Crowned Amazons and the Orange-winged Amazons to name a few. The Amazon parrot is known for its assortment of personality traits and temperaments. Truly, there is an Amazon parrot for just about every kind of bird lover out there.

In this book, you will discover many facts about the Amazon parrot, how to care for it, how to train it, discipline it and deal with certain behaviors, as well as understanding its health risks. The Amazon parrot can live up to sixty years! A lifespan that is lengthy enough to be a lifelong companion. Is it the pet for you? Read on to find out. Who knows, maybe by the end of this book you will be on your way to an avian pet store to get your very own Amazon parrot.

Chapter One: The Exotic Amazon Parrot

One of the most popular bird pets is the parrot. Different species of parrots are kept as companions because of their unique, lovable characteristics: attractive colors, cute mannerisms, impressive intelligence and endearing way of interacting with their owners. A great diversity of this bird can be found in Australasia and South America. Usually, parrot species that are kept as human companions are those from the large breeds such as the amazon, cockatoo, macaw, grey, and eclectus. The most popular in this group is the Amazon Parrot. Amazon parrots originate from Central

Chapter One: The Exotic Amazon Parrot

America, South America and the Caribbean Islands. Wil Amazon parrots can be found in palm groves, rainforests, scrub forests and savannas.

The Amazon parrot is green in color, with different shades on their head ranging from yellow, red, blue, green, lilac and white. There is an estimated 27 species of this parrot, but only about ten to twelve of them are kept as companion pets. Some of the popular members of the Amazon parrot family include the following: yellow - naped Amazon parrot, double yellow-headed Amazon parrot, green-cheeked Amazon parrot, blue-fronted Amazon parrot, mealy Amazon parrot, red - lored Amazon parrot, panama Amazon parrot, white-fronted Amazon parrot, lilacine Amazon parrot, orange-winged Amazon parrot, and the lilac-crowned Amazon parrot.

Young Amazon parrots usually sport a grey-brown iris. The color of their eyes change from red to chestnut brown/ red-orange after about 2 years. Once the color of their iris changes, you can't identify its exact age. They mature sexually at about four to six years of age. However, it is difficult to tell the gender of the Amazon parrot as both female and male look alike. The breeding ability of Amazon parrots is very good, they are compatible with other parrots and they can lay 2 to 4 eggs with an incubation period of only 29 days.

An Amazon parrot typically weighs about 350 to 600 grams. It normally eats seeds, nuts, fruits and even tiny insects. It has an average lifespan of 50 to 60 years. The longest an Amazon parrot has lived, on record, is more than 80 years! It is indeed a bird of longevity. And if you are looking to have one as a pet, you can have it for a very long time, even for the rest of your life!

Why Amazon Parrots are Popular

Amazon parrots love to explore as they are very curious birds with a high intelligence. They have the ability to acquire a large vocabulary and adapt to their environment. Amazon parrots are described as gregarious birds. They are very expressive, extroverted birds that love interaction. They are quite boisterous and playful. They love to strut and flash their tail feathers. Amazon parrots are

Chapter One: The Exotic Amazon Parrot

very vocal communicators that often enjoy singing. Often, these birds can be very noisy. At times, they can be aggressive and display destructive behavior. But once tamed, they can be very charming companion pets.

Amazon parrots are great at expressing themselves either through verbal communication or body language. Even though an Amazon parrot does not know enough words yet to verbalize its expressions, it can raise its head or neck feathers, pin its eyes, broaden its stance and fan its tail feathers to show excitement. It can also be a bit rowdy, and sometimes cute, as it would attempt to wrestle its owners hand using its beak, destroy its wooden toys or swing upside down.

They are amazing talkers and they love music. You will find many Amazon parrots singing their hearts out, as if the song originated from them! They like to make noises, especially to catch the attention of their owners—they can scream, make shrilling sounds, or make honk-like noises.

Amazon parrots are famous for their loyalty and show of affection. They love being with their owners and spending some quality time playing, talking, showing off

Chapter One: The Exotic Amazon Parrot

and having fun. They are quite in demand as pets because they have excellent mimicking capabilities that endear them to many pet owners.

The downside to having Amazon parrots as pets include high maintenance, high cost, and a lot of time needed to provide a safe, comfortable and fun environment where these amazing creatures can thrive. When brought to the right home and to the right owner, they can be the greatest pets.

How Amazon Parrots Communicate

People seem to think that parrots can only echo and they cannot really communicate with people. There have been countless debates over this through the years. But research has shown that Amazon parrots can indeed understand and interpret the behavior of the one communicating to it, and give an appropriate response. When the parrot comprehends the context of the message it can create a message and send one back, either in the same language, or through its gestures.

Chapter One: The Exotic Amazon Parrot

Amazon parrots can produce any kind of sound, they are intelligent that way. They can get the language of what is around them and as they have strong vocal control, they produce sounds and words when they want to get your attention and affection.

Parrots are amazing communicators. While they cannot show their feelings using facial expressions, unlike dogs, they have different ways to express themselves. Moreover, they are sensitive creatures who can recognize, interpret and appreciate behaviors. Here are the different ways your Amazon parrot can be communicating to you:

- *Verbal Communication.* Once it has learned words, your Amazon parrot can use words to tell you how it feels or what it wants. It can mimic noise as well. Your parrot will communicate to you in the language they receive your message. Don't expect your parrot to answer you in English if you don't talk to it in English! Your parrot can use simple words like *Hello, Goodbye, Go, Hungry,* etc. With practice and over time, your parrot can learn more words and even talk to you in phrases or sentences.

Chapter One: The Exotic Amazon Parrot

- *Non-Verbal Communication*: Just as with humans, parrots can show express themselves through body language and sounds. For instance, your parrot can show you it is bored by staying in a corner and not talking. It can also be aggressive and obstinate. It can even show anger by biting or screaming. Your Amazon parrot can make noise when it is trying to get your attention, when it is hurt, or when it is annoyed.

Is the Amazon Parrot the Pet for You?

As with getting any kind of pet, you need to know if it is the right one for you. It will take a lot of commitment, hard work, time, effort and finances to take care of a pet. But if you get the right match, then you will enjoy many happy years with it. How would you know if an Amazon parrot is suited to you?

Chapter One: The Exotic Amazon Parrot

Here are the things you need to consider:

Your lifestyle

Amazon parrots can live for 50 to 60 years. That means you will be responsible for the nutrition, maintenance, and health care of this bird for many decades. If you always go out on long trips, whether for work or pleasure, you need to consider having someone take care of your Amazon parrot while you are away. If you decide to move, you will have to consider its safe transport. Moreover, you need to find and establish a good relationship with a reputable avian vet who will care for your Amazon parrot. Are you up for the challenge? Can your lifestyle support the care of this beautiful bird?

Your time

How much time and attention can you give to your Amazon parrot in terms of caring for it, training it, and interacting with it? You may need at least an hour every day just to spend time with your pet bird, even more when it needs extra care. Add the time you need to clean its home,

Chapter One: The Exotic Amazon Parrot

feed it, etc. You need to consider that your Amazon parrot will require your attention as it wants to entertain you and communicate with you often. Do you have a busy work schedule? How can you fit in the time to interact with your pet?

Your finances

Maintaining an Amazon parrot is costly. On top of the cost of the pet parrot, which can range from $500 to $1000, you will also need roughly $1000 to $1500 annually to keep one. Costs include food, housing, accessories, toys, supplies, food and vet care. The cost will also depend on the health challenges your bird may have.

Available space

Do you have enough space for a large cage? The dimensions of basic cage for this bird would be 81 cm wide, 58 cm deep and 163 cm tall. If you don't have ample space, you can just get a smaller pet.

Chapter One: The Exotic Amazon Parrot

Household impact

You should also consider the people who live with you, if any, should you decide to get an Amazon parrot. Check if they have avian allergies. Are there other pets in the house that can stress your bird? Often, Amazon parrots are possessive and can get jealous of kids. If you have a child and an Amazon parrot, you may not be able to openly show your affection to your child because the bird can get jealous. Similarly, you should check first with your landlord if you can maintain an Amazon parrot in your apartment. Your neighbors may also not like the idea and you can get complaints.

Your capacity for training

Do you like talkative birds? If you don't like noise, then any kind of parrot is not good for you. They can scream or talk loud even during the night or early morning. If you can tolerate a lot of noise, and you love talking, you will love the Amazon parrot.

Chapter One: The Exotic Amazon Parrot

Amazon parrots have strong beaks—you need to be ready to get bitten occasionally, whether by accident or because of aggressive behavior. It won't be easy to train your parrot and even a non-aggressive Amazon parrot can nip you while you are playing.

Your leniency with mischief

Amazon parrots are very mischievous as much as they are clever and energetic. Your pet will wrestle with you, bite perches and destroy toys. If this kind of playfulness is okay with you, go get an Amazon parrot.

Your tolerance for mess

Parrots are messy! Not only do they produce waste frequently, they also like to scatter their food. You will have to line up the cage repeatedly and sweep under the cage often. You will also spend a lot of time washing food and water dishes, toys and the cage. If you can deal with a lot of mess, then the Amazon parrot may be a good pet for you.

Chapter One: The Exotic Amazon Parrot

Your color preference

Do you like green birds? Amazon parrots are generally green. They just have some color highlights on their faces, heads, and around their necks. If you like colorful birds, then don't get the Amazon parrot. If you like green, then this is the bird for you.

There are so many factors to consider, but if you are really decided on getting an Amazon parrot, and all these considerations are well take into account, then you will really enjoy having it for a lifelong companion pet. Read on the succeeding chapters to know more about the habits, behaviors and needs of the Amazon parrot.

Chapter Two: A Home for Your Amazon Parrot

Bird cages come in different sizes and different materials. But the most important factor you need to consider before choosing a home for your bird is this: it is much like selecting a home for yourself or your family. A home should be safe, comfortable, spacious, and complete with "amenities" such as food and water dishes, toys, perches, etc.

Chapter Two: A Home for Your Amazon Parrot

Different Kinds of Bird Cages

- *Stainless steel cages*
    - There are medical-grade and marine-grade stainless steel cages. The most common stainless steel cage used in bird cages is the 304-grade. It is the same kind of steel utilized for utensils and cookware. It is advantageous to get a stainless steel cage of this quality as it is resistant to rust, non-toxic, and easy to clean.

- *Powder-coated cages*
    - These are similar to stainless steel cages because they are made of steel, only with a lower grade. The coating is sprayed on then baked using very high temperatures. This powder coating makes the cage more durable. The only thing you need to worry about is that if you have a very strong-minded parrot, it can chip the paint off by biting.

Chapter Two: A Home for Your Amazon Parrot

- *Metal and plastic cages*
    - If you have a smaller Amazon parrot, then you can get a cage that is made of metal bars with a plastic base. These kinds of cages are easy to clean as you can break the smaller parts down. However, you should be wary of the paint because it is usually pliable and can easily chip.

- *Wooden cages*
    - Wooden cages look just as pretty as plastic cages. However, wood can retain moisture which means bacteria and parasites can grow on it and harm your bird. Furthermore, it is difficult to clean wooden cages. Some wooden cages can look like furniture and can be a great accent to your home. But you should consider that it will be a place where your bird lives and it should have proper ventilation, enough space and is safe.

Chapter Two: A Home for Your Amazon Parrot

- *Acrylic cages*
    - You can choose an acrylic cage for your bird if you want to see your pet more clearly. Similarly, acrylic cages also help tone down the noise. The problem with acrylic cages, no matter how beautiful they look, is that there is not much room for ventilation. Also, there are no bars that your Amazon parrot can climb on. Acrylic cages are expensive.

- *Wrought iron cages*
    - Wrought iron cages look very fashionable. However, the powder-coated ones are much more in demand. This is because the decorative scrollwork in most wrought iron cages can be dangerous for parrots. Additionally, the paint used in wrought iron cages may contain toxic.

- *Ornate cages*
    - Avoid ornate cages. Similar to wrought iron scrollwork, they can be very unsafe for curious parrots.

Chapter Two: A Home for Your Amazon Parrot

Right Size, Right Design

As much as you can, get the largest bird cage to house your Amazon parrot. Birds are meant to fly or roam around (while its wings are clipped). Of course, it is not practical to get a cage that is large enough for your bird to fly around — you would have to have a cage as big as a room! You just need to get a cage where your Amazon parrot can fly, especially if you don't allow your bird out of the cage. You may also need a smaller cage that you can use for traveling with your bird. Get the best cage that your budget and your available space at home can allow.

Remember, your Amazon parrot is not a helicopter. It is best to choose a cage that is longer, not necessarily taller. Your pet needs to pick up flight speed. It's good to choose a horizontal rectangular or -a square cage, not a vertical rectangular one.

Your bird cage should be spacious enough for you to be able to place a hanging rope or play stand, perches and other toys. Make sure that you never scrimp on space, if you want your Amazon parrot to be happy in its home.

Chapter Two: A Home for Your Amazon Parrot

Always check the safety of the cage. Not all are constructed with the well-being of your bird in mind. Check the design, the welds, and the spacing of the bars. Choose a cage whose doors can be lowered down, slid to the side, or opened from the side. Don't get bird cages that can be raised and lowered. Your smart bird can try to open it and may get his head trapped in a guillotine door. There should also be a locking facility on the door so the bird cannot escape.

The food and water dishes should be in the top one-third of the cage, not below the middle. If the cage you get has feeding and watering areas that are placed in the bottom of the cage, then you will have to buy and install new dishes higher in the cage.

Proper Placement

Finding the right spot is essential. You want your pet bird to be healthy physically and mentally. When its home is located in an isolated area, it can get bored or depressed. Similarly, if it is placed in a location that is too noisy, it can become stressed.

Chapter Two: A Home for Your Amazon Parrot

Here is a good checklist you can observe when deciding the best place for your bird cage:

- Make sure there is a lot of traffic, but not too much and too fast. Your family room is a good place to install your bird cage.

- Birds like security so if you can put the cage in the corner of a room, it is ideal.

- Don't place the cage too near the ground. Birds like to have a "bird's eye view" and won't feel secure when they are near the floor.

- The location should not be drafty.

- Avoid placing the cage on a porch as your pet can be stolen by thieves or eaten by predators.

- You should not put your bird cage against a window. Many things that can be viewed from a window can scare your Amazon parrot such as other animals, lightning, etc.

Chapter Two: A Home for Your Amazon Parrot

Accessories for the Bird Cage

Your Amazon parrot's home should be complete so that your pet will enjoy staying in it and live comfortably. Here are some accessories that you can and should put in your parrot's home:

Perches

Perching is crucial for birds. They are not meant to walk on flat surfaces 24 hours a day. You can take care of your bird's feet by letting it perch. By keeping its foot healthy, you are ensuring your bird's well-being. Here are some important tips:

- Make sure to choose different kinds of perches. You can't just have one perch or one kind of perch. It is similar to wearing one pair of shoes day in day out. Your feet will suffer. You can choose wooden perches, made from cholla, cow wood or manzanita. You can also get some clean branches from your yard, as long as they are not sprayed with chemicals. Concrete perches are popular. You can also get plastic perches, as long as it is textured. You should be careful when using rope perches because you don't want your bird to get strangled with loose strings or for it to ingest rope fibers. Look for orthopedic perches as they can help support and fortify the foot muscles of your Amazon parrot.

- The diameter of the perch is also important. You want your bird to be comfortable as well as its foot muscles to be strengthened.

- Keep your perches clean all the time. When the perches are dirty, your Amazon parrot is prone to foot infections.

Bird Toys

A parrot in the wild is naturally active so you should give your captive pet things to do as it resides in its cage. If there is nothing in the cage to occupy your Amazon parrot, it will find something to do like pluck his own feathers out, scream or thrash around his cage. Don't think that your bird is simply being unruly—it could be bored. That is why bird toys are important. Following are some toys you can get for your Amazon parrot:

- Foraging Puzzle. Parrots, like any other bird, love foraging for food. These toys will allow your bird to "solve puzzles" as they figure out how to get food or goodies. Not only does it satisfy their inherent nature of foraging, the puzzle will also provide a physical and psychological challenge for your pet. Your pet's mental health is important.

- Rope toys. Use high-quality rope toys. Usually they are made with soft cotton. It is imperative that your Amazon parrot does not ingest rope material so make sure that there are no loose strands. If your bird gets tied up or tries to ingest the rope toy, remove it immediately.

- Plastic toys. Get toys made from hard plastic or acrylic so that your pet bird won't be able to easily destroy them.

- Wooden toys. Get wooden toys for your bird that it can chew on. When the toy is worn down, take it out of the cage and replace it with a new one. Purchase wooden toys that don't have toxic coloring.

- Preening toys. Parrots love to preen and you can give them toys for this purpose. Preening toys can be made of shredded rope or feathers.

Do not put plush toys in your bird cage as your bird can preen and destroy them. The materials can be ingested by your Amazon parrot and it can get sick or even die.

Cups

If the bird cage you purchased only comes with plastic feeding and drinking dishes, you should purchase stainless steel ones. These are more durable. Moreover, cups made of plastic can be easily scratched and if there are

Chapter Two: A Home for Your Amazon Parrot

crevices in the cups, it is prone to bacterial growth. It is good to get two cups so that while you are cleaning one, you can use the other. While you can use ceramic cups, you need to check them regularly for scratches or chips. You can use hooded cups if your Amazon parrot frequently dumps the food out of the cup.

Lighting

Proper artificial lighting for you bird cage is a necessity, not a luxury, especially if the area does not have natural sunlight. Check with your local pet store for the right lamp or bulb that is perfect for your pet bird.

Cage Covers

While a cage cover is not a necessity, you can purchase one to help protect your bird from draft at night or to allow it to stay quiet later in the morning for some extra sleep for you. You can make it into a nighttime routine with your pet—but it is important to decide early, so that you can be consistent with covering. The cage cover should snugly fit the cage. But you can also use a blanket as a loose cover. You

Chapter Two: A Home for Your Amazon Parrot

just need to be careful when using a loose cover as your Amazon parrot can chew holes in the loose sheet and can strangle your bird.

Even if you really want to use a cage cover, you should consider your bird's response to it. Your bird can be afraid of the dark and may thrash around the cage when you fully cover it. If this is the case, you don't have to cover it entirely, or you can use a night light.

Seed Guards and Bloomers

You can choose a bird cage that has a seed skirt, because your Amazon parrot can be quite messy. You can also opt to buy a cage bloomer to help keep your floors clean. If you can't find a good seed guard or bloomer, you can use a plastic chair mat or a shag rug under your cage. Having a vacuum or broom and dust pan beside the cage will also make cleaning easier.

Chapter Two: A Home for Your Amazon Parrot

Play Stand

There are cages that have play-top gyms installed inside. You can also have a play stand in a separate room or place it beside the cage. You can get a simple one that has a perch and two cups on each end or a complicated one where your bird can climb, alight on orthopedic perches, and play with other bird toys. Don't forget this important thing: you should only leave your Amazon parrot on its play stand when you are there to supervise.

Cleaning Your Amazon Parrot's Cage

It is not easy to clean your bird's cage, but you should not put off cleaning it because it can become crusty and your bird can get sick. To simplify cleaning, you should do it every other day. This will help you avoid the growth of fungus and the accumulation of too much waste and debris. Likewise, you should clean and disinfect your feeding and drinking cups every day.

Chapter Two: A Home for Your Amazon Parrot

Here are more tips for cleaning your bird cage:

- To clean the perches, remove one a day, wash it using hot, soapy water and dry carefully. This way, you prevent your bird's perches from accumulating dirt and bacteria that can be harmful to your parrots feet and general health.

- Check the toys that are in the cage if they are dirty or worn. If they are dirty and soiled, clean them. If torn and worn, throw them away and replace with new ones.

- The cage grate should be removed once a week so you can scrape and wash it.

- Wipe at least one side of your bird's cage each day.

- To clean it thoroughly, you should take your parrot's cage outside the house once a month and pressure clean it. Before you put your bird back in the cage, ensure that it is fully dried.

- Never use a chemical cleaning solution. You can use baking powder if you need to scrub your cage. Make a disinfectant solution by mixing 1 part of bleach with 9 parts of water. Rinse and dry the cage well.

How to Keep Pests Away from the Cage

Many pests can either annoy or dangerously harm your pet Amazon parrot. Here are some:

- Fruit flies. While they may not necessarily harm your pet bird, they can annoy your bird so much. Fruit flies multiply rapidly especially when there are sweet veggies and fruits around. If there is an infestation of flies, remove the veggies and fruits from your bird's diet. Then, place some orange juice in a long-necked bottle so that the fruit flies will dive in and not be able to get out.

- Mites. Red mites, air sac mites and scaly face mites are the common mites that can harm your pet parrot. They can cause itching and restlessness as they hide in your bird's feathers and feed on your bird. Advise your vet immediately once you notice signs of mites. If the mites are too many, your bird can have difficulty breathing. You would need medication to deal with them.

- Seed moths. These are annoying little creatures that feed on the seeds of your parrot and make them webby by laying their eggs. If you are not watchful, multiple eggs can hatch and larvae can grow and invade your whole home. To kill seed moths, you need to freeze all your bird seeds for some days to get rid of the eggs and larva. Make sure to store your bird seed in air-tight containers. In your bird cage, remove all bird seed during night time so that the adult moths can't lay their eggs.

Chapter Two: A Home for Your Amazon Parrot

Chapter Three: Amazon Parrot Nutrition

What can you feed your Amazon parrot? While some people think that birds just need bird seeds or pellets, nothing is further from the truth. Your pet parrot needs variety in order to get a nutritious diet. Your Amazon parrot needs all the nutrients it can get so that it will have healthy feathers, healthy skin and a healthy attitude. The base diet for your pet parrot is balanced food.

Imagine, in the wild, parrots eat a wide range of foods such as fruits, flowers, grass, seeds, nuts, insects, and more. As seasons change, the options for food changes and the

Chapter Three: Amazon Parrot Nutrition

birds in the wild get nourishment from whatever is available in nature for the season.

With a pet parrot at home, you should provide it with natural, whole foods that are also well balanced. If your bird does not have a good diet, it won't become healthy, can't live its full lifespan, and is susceptible to disease and illness. A healthy bird is a happy bird. A bird that does not eat well can also easily get fatigued, bored or depressed. Good nutrition is important for both physical and psychological health.

Base Diet + Supplemental Diet

What you feed your bird primarily is its base diet and the supplemental diet is its snack. Make sure that your Amazon parrot's base diet is as nutritional as possible. Every bite will build the systems in its body and support all the bodily functions. The base diet should be fun to it, because you need to encourage your bird to eat healthy foods. It is offered in the morning as it is usually the time when the

Chapter Three: Amazon Parrot Nutrition

parrot is very hungry. This way, your bird can eat more nutritious stuff. You don't have to limit yourself to bird seeds and bird pellets. Your bird's base diet can include avi cakes, nutria-berries, pellet berries, popcorn nutria-berries, and other foods that you can get in avian retail stores. Many bird food manufacturers have added vegetables and fruits as well as omega fatty acids to bird pellets to make them more healthful.

You can offer your parrot some vegetables and fruits for snacks. Choose the dark green or orange ones as they are more nutritious. You can chop, mash, or grate your vegetables and fruits or you can serve them whole. When you are feeding your parrot with fresh fruits and vegetables, make sure that they stay in the cage or food dish for a short while only. If you leave them there for the rest of the day, or night, it can spoil or get sour and pests will come. Also, you need to rinse the fruits and vegetables well before serving them. If you can get organic fruits and vegetables, it is better. Fruits that you can serve our Amazon parrot include apples, berries, bananas, melon, pineapple and orange. Vegetables include asparagus, carrots, celery, cooked beans, cauliflower, celery, squash, peas, soy beans, peppers, sprouts, yams and leafy greens.

If your bird doesn't want to eat other foods apart from seeds, you may need to give it a dietary supplement. If your bird s is molting, recovering from an injury or sickness, laying eggs or stressed, it won't have much of an appetite and will surely need a dietary supplement to stay healthy. Ask your veterinarian for the best supplement for your bird. You should never over-supplement your bird as it can be harmful to its health. Similarly, if you are using supplement that is added to water, you should change the water supply twice a day and put fresh water with no powder supplement at night. Otherwise, you are inviting bacteria to grow in the water.

Foods to Avoid

Some people think that the following foods are good for their pet parrots, when in fact they are quite unhealthy. It is easy to just grab some cereals while you are having breakfast and hand it over to your parrot to munch on. But too much sugar in those frosted wheats can be bad for the

Chapter Three: Amazon Parrot Nutrition

very small body of your pet bird! Check out the list to find out if you are feeding your Amazon parrot foods that have high sugar content, too much sodium, and unhealthy ingredients.

1. Cereals

   As mentioned earlier, it can be quite tempting to hand out some cereals to your bird, especially if its cage is near the dining area. Cereals should not be the main meal of your Amazon parrot. If you really want to give some crunchy munchies to your pet, go for the ones that have low sugar and low sodium. Go for the plain ones instead of the frosted or fruity ones. Moreover, if you really can't help but give cereal to your bird, give it just a few beak-sized pieces.

2. Microwave popcorn

   While it is crunchy and munch-y and can be a treat for your pet, it is best to pop your own corn kernels instead of getting microwavable ones. Popcorn is a good low-calorie snack, but the microwave variety is

Chapter Three: Amazon Parrot Nutrition

not good for your bird's health. Check out popcorn nutria-berries as they are healthy and more fun alternatives.

3. Granola bars

   It looks healthy, with rolled oats dried fruit and nuts. It can also be a delicious snack for your bird. However, granola bars have very high calorie and sugar content. Some avian stores sell healthy versions of granola bars for birds. Even if you are getting granola bars for yourself, make sure that you get low-calorie, low-sugar ones and only give a beak-size portion to your bird.

4. Wheat bread

   Only give whole wheat bread to your bird. Some bread are packaged as wheat when in truth they only contain a small percentage of wheat flour and is actually processed white bread. Don't give buttered bread to your bird.

Chapter Three: Amazon Parrot Nutrition

5. Dried fruit

   Dried fruits, like prunes, raisins and apricots, are healthy as they have fiber, vitamins, and minerals. But dried fruit is preserved with sulfur dioxide and it is not good for your pet. Purchase unsweetened, unsulfured dried fruit from avian stores as they are naturally fried and persevered. You can include these in your bird's diet.

The Importance of Bird Foraging

Of course you love your pet Amazon parrot and would give it everything. However, you need to remember that birds like, and need, to forage, too. It may be hard for many people to imagine, especially in this day and age when you can call for delivery, get freezer meals that you can just pop in the oven, or go to a drive-thru to get a meal. Understanding the need to work for food is an alien concept. But remember, there are no food cups in the wild. Most birds like to forage—they will search high and low in fields of grasses for seeds or nuts to feed on.

Chapter Three: Amazon Parrot Nutrition

All birds have the instinct to hunt for their own food. But when you freely offer food, you don't encourage the foraging behavior. When birds become too lazy to forage, they can be unhealthy. As it is against their nature, they may also become bored, confused or frustrated. Other birds will become overweight because food is available to them without any hard work.

Many bird food manufacturers have incorporated foraging into their offerings. Nutri - berries, avi cakes and pellet berries are some bird food that encourages healthy foraging behavior. Contrasted with freeloading—or having food readily available—your Amazon parrot will be healthier if it gets food that will require its effort. Foraging puzzles are also helpful when it comes to encouraging your pet to work for its food.

Chapter Four: Good Grooming for Your Amazon Parrot

As with any pet, good grooming is important not just to keep up appearances but to also maintain good health. If you don't groom your Amazon parrot well, it will lose its exquisite appeal. It is fairly easy to groom your parrot, but you will need it to be cooperative so that the grooming process can be safe.

Amazon parrots are tremendously hygienic. They can easily recognize dirt and would want to clean up. Not only do they want their bodies clean, they also want their surroundings tidy. While you have learned tips on how to maintain a clean home for your Amazon parrot in the previous chapters, you should give careful attention to proper grooming such as bathing and beak trimming as well as wing clipping and care during molting.

Beak Trimming

An Amazon parrot's beak is very delicate. Like all other birds, a clean and healthy beak is an indication of the well-being of the bird. In captivity, a parrot's beak must be trimmed. In the wild there is no such concern because Amazon parrots trim their beaks by constantly rubbing them against hard food or trees. When beaks are untrimmed and left to outgrow, Amazon parrots can develop chewing problems. An avian vet can trim the beak of your pet parrot at home or at his clinic. If you want to do it at home, you can do the following:

Chapter Four: Good Grooming for Your Amazon Parrot

- Make sure to wrap your Amazon parrot with a cloth and put a brace on its head so that it can't move while you are trimming its beak.
- Never overdo the trimming as it can cause your bird to suffer an injury and bleed.
- You can use spinning tools instead of filers so that your bird won't get hurt.
- You can also use lava or mineral blocks to gently trim and keep the beak in shape.
- Check the bird's beak for sharp edges after the trimming. If there are some sharp edges, your bird could injure itself.

If you have a new Amazon parrot pet, it is better to leave the beak trimming to professionals so you don't risk injuring your bird.

Wing Clipping

Trimming your pet bird's wings will ensure that it cannot fly out of your home or get injured while flying inside your home. While your bird may initially feel depressed as it cannot fly, you can compensate it by showing

Chapter Four: Good Grooming for Your Amazon Parrot

affection. The procedure is painless, and it is not just important for training but also for good grooming.

If you choose not to clip your bird's wings, for whatever reason, make sure that you have ample space or a really, really large cage that you can place outdoors so your bird can fly around.

Molting

Molting is the shedding of feathers of birds. Amazon parrots molt once or twice every year. Molting is not easy for birds and it can be painful and uncomfortable. When your Amazon parrot is molting, you can ease its condition by misting your bird using warm water so that the growing feathers will become softer. It is important to check your parrot's body for spots or patches. If you notice any unusual feathers or signs of broken ones, bring your Amazon parrot to the avian vet.

When your Amazon parrot feels discomfort and itchiness during molting, bathing will help soothe it. You

Chapter Four: Good Grooming for Your Amazon Parrot

can also hydrate your bird's skin and feathers by spraying distilled aloe vera.

Bathing

Birds love to bath. It is no different with Amazon parrots. They can enjoy daily misting or being lightly sprayed with water. Or they can dip themselves in water that is placed in a shallow dish. Whatever your parrot likes, do it. Most parrots don't like spraying and it is often better to leave a bathing dish so that your pet can go and bathe any time it likes.

The temperature of the bathing water should be room-temperature or cool. Birds want to improve their feather condition and a cool bath does this for them. If the bath water is warm, the oils from their feathers will be stripped off and the Amazon parrots will suffer picking and itching.

Not only does bathing improve the condition of your bird's plumage, it also softens the dirt accumulated on its skin and feathers. Bathing also encourages your Amazon

Chapter Four: Good Grooming for Your Amazon Parrot

parrot to preen. Bathing will wash away the dried droppings, dander and other pollutants and pests such as feather mites. When the pollutants are washed off, there is less chance for your bird to ingest them and become sick. Frequent bathing, according to experts, can boost the respiratory system of your bird.

Here are some bathing tips:

- When misting, use a handheld spray bottle. You will know if your Amazon parrot likes it if it puts its head down, spread its wings wide and shakes around. You can simulate rain shower by misting above your pet parrot's head.

- You can place a shallow bath dish so that your Amazon parrot can wet its feathers or dip its head. This is especially helpful on a warm or hot day, and your bird has access to a bird bath any time it wishes. You can also use a planter saucer. It is not deep and your bird can take a bath in it whenever they feel like jumping it to get wet.

Chapter Four: Good Grooming for Your Amazon Parrot

- Your parrot can also take a shower with you—you need to use a special shower sprayer and perch. If you decide to do this, understand that you need a lot of patience to convince your pet parrot. It needs to trust you and feel safe. You need to make sure that your water is safe by using a shower filter. Chlorine, fluoride and other chemicals can cause respiratory problems for your bird. Not only will it benefit your bird, shower filters are also good to help you maintain the moisture in your hair and skin—something that is taken away with water that has fluoride and chlorine. Shower filters and not expensive and they are not difficult to install at all.

- This is an important advice: never spray a bird that is afraid of it. Do not force your bird to like spraying or misting. Instead offer other bath alternatives.

- Never blow dry your Amazon parrot. Your bird can dry itself and it can regulate its own eat. Not only will you scare your bird with the heat and sound, but the chemical from the non-stick coating in the blow dryer can harm your bird. Exposure to the sun will help your Amazon parrot to dry after a bath.

- If your bird, surprisingly, does not like bathing, you can entice it to go for a bath by placing a flat dish with wet greens like kale, watercress, or spinach. It won't immediately like to bath, but if you are consistently offering this wet dish with greens, you will encourage your bird to get wet and love the feeling. Soon it will be bathing on its own.

- You should never use soap when bathing your bird. Only when in dire circumstances, like when your parrot's feathers have oil, can you use soap to wash it off—and you can only use mild glycerin soap and wash its body and not its face. You should also not scrub it. Then you have to rinse carefully. You should be gentle when giving your bird a bath.

Chapter Four: Good Grooming for Your Amazon Parrot

When the weather is cool, you should keep baths to a minimum. When the weather is warm, you can completely soak your parrot and it's okay. You can use a bird lamp to dry your parrot.

Chapter Four: Good Grooming for Your Amazon Parrot

Chapter Five: Training Your Amazon Parrot

While there is no doubt that you will enjoy the beauty and splendor of your Amazon parrot even as it stays in its cage—watching it feed and play—you will unleash more of its potential by training it. They are far more than just caged pets, they can be interesting companions. Your Amazon parrot can even be your friend.

In the Beginning

As with any new pet that is brought into a home, the first few days can either be a bit stressful or easy for both the Amazon parrot and its owner, and this is all dependent on

Chapter Five: Training Your Amazon Parrot

the age, personality, previous habitat of the bird as well as how it is introduce to its new home. The good news is that birds are very easy-going and adaptable animals and if you make its new home comfortable enough, your Amazon parrot will easily settle in.

Even though you are quite excited to spend time with this intelligent, sociable bird, you should give it several hours of "alone time" after you place it in its new home. Playing with it immediately can stress it out. The bird should be accustomed to its new home and be able to locate its food and water sources as well as perches and toys. Ensure that the perches are placed correctly and securely, the food and water dishes are kept clean and within easy reach, and the location of the cage is safe. As you watch your bird go around its new home, you can identify if there are things you need to adjust to make your Amazon parrot more comfortable and out of harm's way.

It is important to get to know your bird before you start interacting with it. Younger Amazon parrots have outgoing personalities and are more extroverted than older ones and would immediately want to play with you. If your

Chapter Five: Training Your Amazon Parrot

Amazon parrot came from a rescue facility, you may want to give it extra time to get used to its new surroundings, as it is not used to hands-on play. Make sure to observe your Amazon parrot to get to know it, what it likes and what it doesn't like. There may be toys it is afraid of, or food that it doesn't like. Maybe it loves to sing or talk, maybe it doesn't like to play too much. You have to remember, not all Amazon parrots are alike. Just as it is with people, every bird has a different personality.

It's All about Trust

Everything begins with trust—and the same is true with taming and training pets. When your Amazon parrot trusts you and realizes that you are not out to harm it, you will not have a hard time making it sit on your shoulder, feed from your hand, or play with you.

The first and most important practice is using your hands. Repeated handling, touching and fondling on your Amazon parrot's head, face, back of the neck, feet and under the wings will show your bird that you care for it. It will get

Chapter Five: Training Your Amazon Parrot

used to your touch and your presence. It will help you build a connection. When you have this attachment, it will be easy to teach your bird new tricks.

Similarly, talking to your bird will help establish a connection. If you are not much of a communicator and you think that having a pet is simply about giving them food, water and toys, and watching them, then you and your pet are going to be disappointed. Having a companion pet means taking the time to communicate; birds such as the Amazon parrot like to talk—and guess what, they expect their owner "friends" to talk back to them. You should relate to your parrot using gentle gestures and words spoken in a soothing manner.

Before Taming and Training

There are basic rules that must be followed before you can begin to tame and train your new Amazon parrot. Apart from ensuring that you have a good home for it, you must have its wings clipped. Do not worry, clipping the Amazon

Chapter Five: Training Your Amazon Parrot

parrot's wings is not a painful procedure. The main flight feathers are cut short to ensure that the bird can be confined in the safety of your home. The Amazon parrot is left with the ability to lift itself enough to float to the ground from an elevated place. Wing clipping also facilitates the taming and training process. A good vet will be able to do a painless procedure wherein there will be no discomfort or bleeding.

It is inherent for birds to fly around, and you don't want your bird to hurt itself by crashing onto windows, ceilings or cabinets in your home when you let it out of its cage. Moreover, it will be easier to tame and train a bird that cannot fly away as you teach it. While training, you can prevent your Amazon parrot from injury by keeping a carpeted area or making the "fall" areas softer and prevent a crash landing. Also, avoid placing its cage on very high places.

You already know how to provide the best home for your Amazon parrot from the previous chapters. Make sure that the cage has a large door. This will allow you to easily get your Amazon parrot out when it is time to train. Once your pet is trained, you only need to let the door open and

Chapter Five: Training Your Amazon Parrot

you can coax it to go out or it will go out on its own. That is why you need to door to be wide enough so that the Amazon parrot won't get hurt going out.

Lighting and sound can affect training big time. You cannot expect your parrot to be able to grasp what you are teaching it in a noisy environment. It will be easily distracted and can even be afraid. Similarly, an environment that is too bright can be distracting for both you and your parrot. Make sure that training time is quiet time—it should be a calm, peaceful environment. One that speaks "I am here for you, I am your friend. Don't be afraid. You will not get hurt."

As with the soothing lighting and quiet environment, your voice and actions should also be gentle. This will cause your bird to trust you. The way you speak and move should communicate that you are careful and that you mean your bird no harm. Think of it as handling a small baby. For instance, when you bring the bird out of the cage for training, be sure to handle it gently and not too tightly. When you do this, your bird will have a pleasant experience and won't be too afraid of you holding it the next time. Your touch and your voice should be reaffirming. When it goes on

Chapter Five: Training Your Amazon Parrot

the floor, get it by using cupped hands and gently lifting it up by its breast, not from its back or neck. Your hands should feel like a sanctuary to it. Remember, you want your Amazon parrot to trust you, like you and consider you a friend. As mentioned earlier, rust is vital.

To summarize, you need to remember the following before you start training:

- The flight wings of the Amazon parrot are clipped.
- Your cage should have a large door so you can easily get it out or it can easily come out when needed.
- Training sessions should be done in a quiet environment with subdued lighting.
- You should talk in a calm, soothing voice.
- You should move slowly and be gentle.
- You should not hold your Amazon parrot too tightly.

Taming a New Amazon Parrot

Once the wings of your new Amazon parrot has been clipped, the environment is conducive and you know how to use a gentle voice and touch, you can begin taming. The next

Chapter Five: Training Your Amazon Parrot

thing you need your Amazon parrot to know, after it realizes it can trust you, is that you (your hands, shoulder, lap) and its cage are safe places.

While in the cage, you can gently touch and caress your Amazon parrot on the back of its neck or its head. When it goes away from you, just use your hand to gently touch it again. When it is used to our touch inside the cage, you can softly carry it out of the cage and place it on your arm or your shoulder. Let it sit or walk, while you gently touch it in its head, belly or feet. If it escapes from you, tenderly pick it up and place it back. Do this regularly with your bird, until you see that it stays close to you or doesn't mind your touches. Even when its flight feathers grow back, it will still know that perching on you and staying in its cage is still safe. As it flies around, it will still naturally land on you or on its cage.

Training a Shy Amazon Parrot

Your Amazon parrot can have a shy personality—and it is okay. You can still train it. How do you know that it is a

Chapter Five: Training Your Amazon Parrot

shy bird? By observing it! It may withdraw from you or not be responsive when you are training it or talking to it, but when it shows interest in what is going on around its surroundings and you when your attention is not on it, then it could simply be shy. Your Amazon parrot may not be used to contact with people and can be initially contented to stay in its cage, even as it is comfortable having you around in the same room. It can even be watching what you do, even if it goes to the back of its cage when you come near. Don't worry—your Amazon parrot could still be looking for an indication that you are not scary and you have no intention of hurting it. It is a good sign when you offer your Amazon parrot a snack and it takes it from you, even if it is hesitant at first. That means that your bird wants to work with you.

If the Amazon parrot you brought home is shy like this, you will have to make it used to your presence before you begin training or exacting demands on it. To make your bird comfortable to you, you can offer it food or water by moving your hand close to it and yet not touch it when you put food and water in its dishes; avoid eye contact and just

Chapter Five: Training Your Amazon Parrot

speak gently to your parrot. This way, you are near and yet avoiding contact—you won't scare your bird away. Soon it will be conditioned to your presence.

When you feel that it is used to having you near it, then try to touch your Amazon parrot's head or chest gently, and slowly pull your hand away. This will give your bird the impression that your touch is not dangerous or something to be scared of. When your bird feels that your touch is enjoyable and comfortable, it will allow you to touch it more. Soon, it won't be shy in your presence anymore. Pretty soon, you can experiment on scratching your Amazon parrot on its head, or making it perch on your finger.

It can be a different experience for every owner and bird—some birds are more shy and withdrawn than others, some owners are more patient than others. Make sure to take the process very slowly if your notice that your bird is shy so that you can avoid being bitten by your Amazon parrot. Moreover, you should not show any fear towards your bird or it will think it is more dominant than you and not follow any of your leading in the future. Furthermore, do your best

Chapter Five: Training Your Amazon Parrot

not to demand your bird to act the way you want it to respond.

Taming a Fearful Amazon Parrot

A shy Amazon parrot is different from a fearful one. The fearful parrot does not want to be touched. There are a number of reasons why a parrot can be fearful: it could have been raised by its parents in the wild, it could be a rescued bird that has no idea of any human interaction, it could be a breeder bird, or it could have had a negative experience when it came to people touching it. Regardless of the reason why your bird is fearful, you can gain its trust by building its confidence in the new home with you.

How can you differentiate if your Amazon parrot is shy or fearful? If it simply withdraws, but keeps on observing you, it is shy, as mentioned above. However, if it keeps on thrashing around its cage when you or another person enters the room and look afraid, then it is more than shy. A fearful Amazon parrot can freeze in place and stay very still in the hopes that humans won't notice it. Other

Chapter Five: Training Your Amazon Parrot

fearful parrots can exhibit aggressive behavior such as clicking beaks, hissing or making other sounds so that humans will go away.

If your Amazon parrot is fearful, you can handle it as you would a shy Amazon parrot, only you need to be more cautious, gentler and more patient. It may take a longer time and more effort to tame a fearful bird. So that you won't risk being bitten, you can use stick training instead of using your hands to be near your bird. Remember never to use gloves as they make birds more afraid. You need to make the bird more accustomed to seeing your hand.

If you feel that your bird is fearful, it will take a longer time for it to be accustomed to its new home, so don't worry about backing off and letting your Amazon parrot eat and drink peacefully. You will know that you can start getting closer when it does not draw back and become as still as stone when you are in the same room. When it appears to be comfortable having you around, it can even go near you when you are near the cage placing food and water.

Chapter Five: Training Your Amazon Parrot

Regardless if your bird is shy or fearful, you should approach taming gradually. Remember, the idea is to introduce yourself to your Amazon parrot as a friend — someone it can be comfortable with and someone it can trust.

Training your Amazon Parrot to Talk

There are many bird species that can imitate human speech as well as many other sounds, and the most popular of them is the parrot. After taming your Amazon parrot, the next thing you can teach it is to talk. Its natural ability can be enriched as you spend time talking, singing or whistling to it. It will learn more quickly as you spend more time with it. You can start teaching it by repeating its name during the times you feed it. It is important to plan your training routine. Training your Amazon parrot to talk requires short, frequent sessions. It can be done in the morning and afternoon, or as much as five times a day, if you have time. Talking lessons should only take 2 to 4 minutes as birds have very short attention span.

Chapter Five: Training Your Amazon Parrot

Here's a good tip: It is best to choose a name for your Amazon parrot that has an "ee" sound that is connected with a harsh consonant, like Nina, Peter, or Betty. When it has learned to repeat its name, you can teach it your name, or simple words or greetings like "Hello", "Bye bye" or "Good night". You should also encourage good behavior that will arouse speech—do it using baby steps. Using tones will allow your pet to imitate words. That is why whistling is a good technique, because you are teaching your bird to make or imitate sounds.

You can teach your Amazon parrot to talk while it is on its cage, or you can hold it when you teach it. Perch the bird on your forearm and place it in front of your mouth to get its attention. As you are close to your bird, not only are you gaining its focus but you are also deepening your connection.

Another good technique you can use to encourage your Amazon parrot to talk is to have someone else with you, like a friend or relative. The Amazon bird can learn better and will have a greater desire to "speak up" as it is challenged by a seeming "rival" in communicating with you.

Chapter Five: Training Your Amazon Parrot

Moreover, your Amazon parrot will learn to speak as it observes your interaction with another speaker.

Movement can be associated with words or phrases. When you are teaching your bird action words or phrases, it is important to do something associated with the words you teach. For instance, you want it to learn the word "Up", then lift your bird high as you repeat "Up".

Teaching your Amazon parrot to talk should be fun, for both you and your parrot. One of the best ways is to show excitement when you talk, so that your bird will associate it with enjoyment. You can also do a reward system, where you give your bird treats when it repeats the word you are teaching it. Rewarding a pet—any kind of pet, for that matter—should be done immediately after the required behavior is exhibited by the pet. Any later and the bird won't associate the reward with doing something correctly. Likewise, when your Amazon parrot is not taking, do not give in to the desire to give it a treat to coax it. As it longs for the treat, it will have a greater yearning to perform.

Chapter Five: Training Your Amazon Parrot

Remembering that each bird has an individual personality, you need to experiment on what you teach your bird and how to communicate with it. You can try to teach it other things apart from greetings if it is not that kind of bird. You can teach it to sing, if that is its inclination.

Other people record the words they want their birds to learn and play the recordings. You can do this too, but you need to limit it to not more than five minutes during teaching time. Prolonged exposure to the recording can bore your bird and even cause it to be stressed. Again, remember that a personal connection with you is the best way it can learn.

As with any kind of training, the owner/trainer should be very patient. Some birds learn fast, others not so. Your Amazon parrot may learn to speak in just a few months, or it can do so after a few years. Respect your bird. Do not punish it for not talking, and do not show anger, annoyance or frustration if it doesn't respond immediately. When you respect the pace in which it learns and acts in response to your training, your Amazon parrot will respect you in return.

Chapter Five: Training Your Amazon Parrot

Stages of Talking

Your Amazon parrot will enjoy talking to you and talking with you, it may even sing! But as with very young children, your pet won't start to talk on the first day you teach it. There are different stages of talking, when it comes to birds. Depending on your style of teaching and the personality of your bird, it can take a few weeks or some years to go from one stage to another. You need to understand them before you start teaching your bird to "talk":

The first stage is the stage of *interest*. Your Amazon parrot will be willing to get your attention as well as your affirmation. It may not immediately understand what you are saying, but it can understand your behavior. When you show acknowledgment and reward it when it mimics the sounds you make, it will learn to show interest in the practice. This stage can progress in one week.

The second stage is when the parrot starts to *bobble words*. Because the parrot is new to it or it lacks practice and control over its vocals, it won't be easy for it to "speak out". As a trainer, you should exhibit much patience. Continue to

Chapter Five: Training Your Amazon Parrot

encourage your parrot to talk by continually sounding out a simple word to it. If you feel frustrated when your parrot is taking a long time to mimic you, do not be angry with it or show frustration or aggression. Your parrot will be discouraged and stop practicing.

The third stage starts when the parrot can repeat a *clear single word.* Keep in mind that your pet bird can only learn one word at a time. Do not make it confusing by teaching so many words at once. It will only cause your parrot to utter meaningless sounds as everything gets mixed up. Repeat the same sound over and over again until your parrot gets it, before you move on to a new sound or word.

The fourth stage is *fluent learning.* When your Amazon parrot has learned a word and is repeating it with ease, you will soon see it progress to speaking more words and even communicating with you verbally. Don't get overly excited and start teaching a lot. Do the same technique and teach your pet one word at a time.

Chapter Five: Training Your Amazon Parrot

Training your Amazon Parrot to "Step Up"

Teaching your Amazon parrot to "step up" is crucial. Not only will it strengthen your bond, it can also save your parrot's life. The "step up" trick is easy to teach—your bird will step up onto your finger or your hand. While birds can naturally perch, you need to teach "step up" to your pet parrot.

To teach your parrot to "step up", do the following:

1. Place your Amazon parrot in a perch. You can also let it perch on one of your fingers. Make sure that your bird is not standing on a flat surface when you teach "step up".

2. Apply mild pressure on your parrot's lower belly or chest so that it will be off balance. Once your Amazon parrot feels out of balance, it will lift one foot.

3. Put your finger under the lifted foot, and lift it higher in a gentle manner. Then say, "Step up". You need to lift your finger otherwise your bird will not

Chapter Five: Training Your Amazon Parrot

understand the concept of moving onto your finger and just leave it's other foot on the perch it was originally standing on.

4. Repeat the instruction until your bird steps up with both of its feet onto your finger.

5. Do this repeatedly for a few times each day. This way your bird will understand that the instruction "step up" means it needs to stand on your finger or hand.

While this trick is simple enough to teach, you need to remember some crucial things. One, your finger or hand where your pet parrot will "step up" onto needs to be sturdy. You should not falter by being nervous; otherwise your Amazon parrot will feel your unease and be anxious as well. Should you wobble or drop your Amazon parrot, it will not climb onto your finger or hand again, trying to avoid the same feeling or incident. If you insist, it could even bite you. That is why you should, in the beginning, make sure that your hand is sturdy and steady. Another thing, you

Chapter Five: Training Your Amazon Parrot

should use both hands when teaching "step up". If you only use one hand, your bird will associate the command with it alone and be wary of stepping up onto the other hand. Keep in mind that your Amazon parrot, like all birds, is a creature of habit. You need to teach one trick using different scenarios. When your pet parrot has mastered the art of stepping up, you can have your family and friends do the same with it, provided that they are confident and have a steady hand.

Stick Training Your Amazon Parrot

Stick training is as easy as "step up" — only this time, you will use a stick or a dowel as a perch instead of your hand. If you have an Amazon parrot that is shy or that keeps on biting, you should train it using a stick first instead of your hand.

First thing you need to do is to choose dowels or sticks that are differently shaped. Always use sticks that have varying textures and colors. Do not use smooth, slick

Chapter Five: Training Your Amazon Parrot

sticks. You can use two or three, just make sure to include one that is very long. Why do you need a long stick? If for some reason, you need to retrieve your Amazon parrot from a high spot, you can easily do so using a long stick if your bird is already stick-trained.

Some birds will naturally step onto a dowel or stick as they would your hand. But others will be wary or scared of sticks and you need to condition them to getting used to it. To acclimatize your bird to sticks, you can bring them near its cage, about a few feet, and gradually move them closer day by day. When you notice that your Amazon parrot has been used to seeing sticks place them inside or on top of its cage. When your pet is not afraid anymore, it will touch the stick. At this point, you will find it easy to make your Amazon parrot step onto your stick.

When your bird already knows how to step up onto the stick, you can try "laddering" — you will ask your bird to step on the stick from your hand, then to your hand from the stick, and so on. Let it be a game that you do a couple of times a day. Do it for only a few minutes so that it won't be boring or tiring for your pet.

Chapter Five: Training Your Amazon Parrot

Potty Training your Amazon Parrot

Sounds funny? Your Amazon parrot can actually be potty trained! There are many ways to teach your parrot such as verbal cues and physical cues. Verbal cues include the following: "Business", "Bombs away" or "Go poop". Watch your bird and whenever you see that it is going to let loose, excitedly speak out your chosen cue. As soon as the poop falls, praise your bird. As you always do this, your Amazon parrot will associate your verbal cue with the action. Soon, it will "go poop" when you tell it to.

You can also use physical cues such as placing a piece of paper for it to let go on. As with verbal cues, you need to stand by and wait for your bird to go then, catch its poop with your paper then praise your bird. When you do this regularly, the Amazon parrot will associate your action of placing a paper beneath it as a cue to do its business. You can combine physical and verbal cues.

As with children, potty accidents can happen. Do not scold or punish your pet. It may or may not be able to pick up your cues quickly. Similarly, do not potty train your bird so strictly that it will only do its business when you say so. It can cause your Amazon parrot to hold its waste in and can possibly get sick. Even if your goal is to potty train your bird, it should be allowed to do its business on its own in or around its cage.

Using Positive Reinforcement in Training

Using positive reinforcement when training pets is common for dogs, but you can also use it you're your pet birds. Amazon parrots are intelligent birds and they will certainly respond to this kind of training. You will disregard negative behavior and reward positive ones. Use this kind of training for your pet parrot to easily identify what kind of behavior you expect from it. Rewards can be in the form of treats or a show of affection.

Have you heard of "quiet time" discipline for children? Do you know that you can also use it with parrots? For instance, you don't like your Amazon parrot to scream.

Chapter Five: Training Your Amazon Parrot

Unless of course your pet is injured or sick, then screaming is an unwanted behavior. When you scream back at your parrot telling it to stop, you are giving it attention and it won't understand that you dislike the behavior. Instead of reprimanding it, it is better that you ignore it and leave it to itself. On the other hand, when your parrot is being quiet, reinforce this good behavior by giving it a positive response. Tell it "Good quiet" so that it will understand that being quiet is a good behavior. Make sure you are consistent with this and pretty soon, your bird will realize that screaming won't get him attention.

Use positive reinforcement for any kind of behavior you want to influence.

More Tricks?

There are a variety of tricks and behaviors you can teach your Amazon parrot—there is really no limit to what it can learn. As long as you have a lot of free time and you are patient and creative with your teaching methods, your pet parrot can do anything. Amazon parrots love to show off

Chapter Five: Training Your Amazon Parrot

and be admired. They are very intelligent and quite interactive. Do not think about getting an Amazon parrot and just leave it its cage. It will be a waste of the amazing talents of this wonderful bird.

Chapter Six: Can You Discipline an Amazon Parrot?

In the previous chapter, positive reinforcement was mentioned as a way to encourage training. But it is utterly impossible to punish an Amazon parrot, or any parrot for that matter, in the literal sense of the word. It is punishment for a bird when it doesn't get what it wants. For example, it desires attention and you don't give it time, then it will "feel" chastised. However, you need to understand that they don't see it as punishment—and you can train and discipline a parrot through creating a habit. Most birds are creatures of

Chapter Six: Can You Discipline an Amazon Parrot?

habit and instinct. So if you want it to create a good habit, then make sure that they don't get what they want when they show bad behavior and give them what they want when they show good behavior. When you do so, they will learn.

Over the years, people have mistakenly practiced punishments to their pet birds. They fail to realize that these actions don't work at all. Learn some of them — so you don't do it to your Amazon parrot:

- Spraying your parrot with water.
    - This action does not feel like a punishment for birds. For one, they will think it's time for bath, an activity that they enjoy. For another, they might become afraid of water, or develop a strong dislike for it, especially if they have been sprayed too strongly. While the shock of being sprayed may immediately stop the behavior you dislike, your Amazon parrot

Chapter Six: Can You Discipline an Amazon Parrot?

won't learn anything with the action and will just repeat the behavior in the future.

- Flicking your bird's beak.
    - Never, ever flick your bird's beak. It is a very sensitive part of its body. You should treat your bird with respect. Imagine someone flicking your nose too strongly. Would you like that? When you gently tap your bird's beak to show affection, it is okay.

- Dropping or wobbling the bird.
    - Some owners "punish" their birds for biting by dropping it. That is wrong. You can seriously hurt your bird, and it won't even think that it is a punishment. If you want to wobble your bird away to avoid a bite, you can do so, but do it lightly. You can also gently drop the bird, to teach it not to bite.

Chapter Six: Can You Discipline an Amazon Parrot?

- Using quiet time or time out.
    - While time out is applicable when it comes to negative reinforcement, it is ineffective when you don't praise the bird for the exhibiting good behavior, like being quiet instead of screaming.

- Using violence.
    - Any form of violence is not acceptable. It is animal abuse! When you are violent with your Amazon parrot, or any kind of pet, you are teaching it to be afraid of you.

Instead of thinking of ways to chastise your Amazon parrot for their bad behavior, you should be on the lookout for good behavior and be ready to praise. Remember, birds don't understand punishment as humans do. So it won't work with them. Allow your bird to create good habits and positive responses based on its instincts.

Love, patience and encouragement is the best form of discipline for your Amazon parrot. Use praise words to

Chapter Six: Can You Discipline an Amazon Parrot?

hearten your bird during training. You should also be able to identify what kind of behavior is good or bad. For instance, biting your hand is not acceptable. But biting things that are placed around the bird's cage can be acceptable. In fact, it is necessary for parrots to do so as it will help sharpen their beaks. Training and discipline, then, is largely dependent on the wisdom of the owner.

Dealing with Behavior

Your Amazon parrot may exhibit different behaviors—some of it is natural, while some are destructive. It is important that you understand what your parrot is acting out so you can handle it properly.

Preening

Preening is the action of birds in which they keep their feathers appear clean. By preening, they maintain their feathers in flying condition and make it waterproof. You will notice that your Amazon parrot is bothering or ruffling its

Chapter Six: Can You Discipline an Amazon Parrot?

feathers using its beak. No, it is not itching; it is preening to make its feathers become neat. It is important for a bird's survival and mating. When it bothers its feathers, it is taking out debris. As it preens, the parrot breaks up the feathers that are powdered-down—feathers that are growing close to its skin—and makes them insulated and waterproof.

Usually your Amazon parrot will preen itself after meals and after a bath. When it shakes its feathers out, a cloud of powder or dust will come from the bird's body. If you have two or more parrots in a cage, you will notice that they will pair up and preen each other. Allo-preening, as paired preening is called, strengthens the bond between birds as they help each other stay tidied up.

If you don't see your parrot preening, then it may be suffering from an illness or is experiencing discomfort in its cage. When your parrot isn't well-groomed as it has stopped preening itself, it is best to ring it to an avian vet immediately.

Chapter Six: Can You Discipline an Amazon Parrot?

Body Language

When your Amazon parrot bites, do not immediately think that it is a behavior problem. It could be hurt or scared. Maybe it does not want you to go near it. You need to understand what your bird is telling you with its body language. Some actions include:

- Flaring of tail: Your parrot can be excited. The flaring of its tail feathers is a different action compared to preening.

- Pining of the eye: When your parrot's pupils are dilated, they are excited. You may want to keep your fingers and hand to yourself during this time as your parrot may bite out of excitement.

- Clicking of beak: This can be a sign of both excitement and warning. When it does not want you to come close, it will make a sound using its beak to ward you off.

Chapter Six: Can You Discipline an Amazon Parrot?

- Fluffing of feathers: A bird that is cold or ill will try to keep itself warm by fluffing its feathers.

- Flapping of wings: Birds that are happy flap their wings. It can also be a sign that they are getting ready for flight.

- Wiping of its beak: There is no bad behavior here. Your bird is just cleaning its beak after eating.

- Shivering: Shivering can be a sign of excitement and it can also be a sign that your bird is feeling cold. The breast muscles shiver as they contract and expand in order to produce body heat.

- Shaking of the head: There is no bad behavior associated with this action. Often parrots shake their heads to remove something they feel in their ears. Shaking heads is a normal behavior.

Chapter Six: Can You Discipline an Amazon Parrot?

- Bobbing of the head. Anxious parrots bob their heads as they want to go someplace else. It can also be a sign that your pet is getting your attention as it wants to bond with you.

Plucking

Plucking or chewing off its feathers is an issue of a parrot when it is sick or as a bad habit. You need to identify the cause for this behavior so you can address it properly. First thing you can do is get a medical evaluation. An Amazon parrot may pluck its feathers because it feels bad due to an infection or skin problem. When parrots suffer from respiratory infections they will pluck their feathers on their chest and leg. If there is no underlying medical condition, you should check the surroundings of your bird.

There can be environmental factors that cause this behavior such as dry air or a change in environment that causes stress like the presence of balloons, new artwork, new carpet, a computer or a new person in the house. You may have to give your bird extra baths or misting to keep its skin moist if the problem is dry air. Or you should remove the stressors that are causing it to feel bad.

Moreover, you should check your bird's diet. Poor nutrition can cause it to pluck its feathers. Your Amazon parrot may need vitamin supplements and a protein boost. You should also encourage it to forage as it will improve its mental health and reduce boredom.

Being "One - Person Birds"

Some parrots that are in captivity have a tendency to become "one-person birds" meaning they only bond with one person and will shun out everybody else, be stressed when there are other people, or be aggressive to those that are not its person. This is normal behavior although not many people understand or accept it, especially for couples. Some birds can even change their alliances as years go by. They may suddenly prefer the other person in the household and shun their original person. You couldn't tell what happens in this bird's brain!

Chapter Six: Can You Discipline an Amazon Parrot?

You can't choose who your bird will like, but you can influence its behavior and prevent this "one-person" thing from happening. Have different types of people handle your bird, especially if you have a big family, let all of them give your Amazon parrot equal attention. Most Amazon parrots are very friendly and you won't have to worry about your pet having thins condition.

Your Amazon Parrot's Behavior Can Be Affected by Hormones

It is not only humans that are affected by their hormones—even birds moods and behaviors can be influenced by the chemical imbalance in their bodies. Once a year, mature Amazon parrots can become hormonal, especially when natural light or day is longer than night. Birds are photosensitive creatures and they feel the change in the cycle of light. Most birds will become loud and aggressive, while others will be sullen and sad. Other parrots lay eggs, even when they don't have a mate! This is a

Chapter Six: Can You Discipline an Amazon Parrot?

reason why owners mistake hormonal behavior with mating behaviors.

If you see that your Amazon parrot is exhibiting hormonal behavior, do your best to prevent nest building. You may have a bird that will try to bite you in an aggressive stance of protecting its nest so you should also be careful. To help regulate its hormones, you can control the amount of light it is exposed to. Once the seasons change, the hormonal behavior will dispel and everything will return to normal.

Dealing with Your Amazon Parrot

Yes, they are birds but they are creatures that think and feel. It is not right to just bring a bird into your home and expect it to entertain you. They are sensitive creatures, and quite intelligent enough to pick up the mood or the vibes in their surroundings. They will do their best to fit in within the household they are brought into.

Chapter Six: Can You Discipline an Amazon Parrot?

Now if you think that you can get an Amazon parrot and expect it to entertain you with its tricks and all, then you got it all wrong. You get a pet so that you can care for it, so that it can be your companion not a toy. If you treat your pet as an equal, someone you respect, then you will receive the same treatment. When it comes to taming, training or handling your Amazon parrot, in the beginning treat it as a child that needs your direction, care and guidance. But also expect your pet bird to mature—and they do mature quickly. After acclimating and training, when you treat your Amazon parrot as you would an adult, you will enjoy a beautiful relationship with it.

Living with a bird is not as easy as living with a pet dog or cat, they are much easier to take care of. As an owner, you will put its needs first to ensure that it will thrive in its environment. Birds are more physically fragile than furry four-legged creatures. In addition to that, they are emotionally and mentally delicate, too. While they can adapt easily, they will also be easily agitated and saddened when they are ignored or when their owner treats them poorly.

Chapter Six: Can You Discipline an Amazon Parrot?

As you decide to get an Amazon parrot for a pet, that decision should come with a commitment to spend ample quality time with your bird so that your relationship will strengthen. Do you know that when wild parrots mate, they mate for life? The same is true for captive ones—they are hard-wired to stick to you, want your attention and affection, as well as love you for a long time. So don't disregard them. If you want good behavior, you need to invest time and affection.

Chapter Seven: Caring for Your Bird's Health and Getting the Right Vet

Your Amazon parrot can live for as long as sixty years if you keep it healthy and strong. Like all animals, parrots are prone to many common illnesses, but these diseases can be avoided when you are watchful and you know how to care for your beloved pets. Read on to find out more about parrot diseases, learn symptoms so that you can go to the vet immediately, and get tips on how you can care better for your Amazon parrot at home.

Chapter Seven: Caring for Your Bird's Health and Getting the Right Vet

Respiratory Infections

Mold in your bird cage can cause fungal growth that can cause various respiratory problems for your Amazon parrot and even bring about nutritional deficiencies. One such case is aspergillosis—a disease that can prove fatal to your bird as it affects the respiratory tract and other organs in your bird's body. When your bird inhales spores, infection can occur. These infections can cause lesions in the lungs and other organs. A surgery may be required to help your bird.

Mold can grow in straw or water dishes (or wooden cages). It is best to always clean the cage as well as the water and food dishes. You can also ask your veterinarian for vaccinations.

Chapter Seven: Caring for Your Bird's Health and Getting the Right Vet

Viral Diseases

Viruses are airborne and it is not easy to control or isolate your parrot that has a viral infection, especially when you have multiple parrots at home. Some viruses like polyoma are deadly and if they infect your baby bird, your pet can die within 24 to 48 hours. Ask your vet for a vaccine to help avoid viral infections.

Bacterial Infections

Amazon parrots are also prone to bacterial infections such as Strep, Citrobacter, Staph and E. coli. Bacteria can come from seeds, water, old food, wet cages, dusty pots or humid areas. If your bird has a weak immune system, it can be susceptible to bacterial infection. You will notice that a bird with an infection will have green or watery droppings. The bacteria can come via inhalation which can result in sneezing, coughing, swelling of the eye, excessive swallowing and rubbing of the eye. The bacteria can affect the kidneys, liver and bowel of your pet. It can be life-threatening so it is important to immediately consult a vet

Chapter Seven: Caring for Your Bird's Health and Getting the Right Vet

once you see signs and symptoms. This way, you can get proper treatment. If you don't prefer antibiotics and want to opt for natural remedies, always consult with your vet first.

Additionally, if the vet says that a bacterial infection is present, you should remove the grit, food and seed from the cage and disinfect everything from cage to accessories to food and water dishes. The bacteria can also be in the old food. A bird being treated and recovering from bacterial infection should not be let out of its cage.

Nutrient Deficiencies

Your bird needs balanced nutrition and if there is an imbalance in its diet, it can lack in the needed vitamins and minerals. Some illnesses that can arise include Vitamin A deficiency, hyperthyroidism, obesity, fatty liver syndrome, and diabetes. It is important to provide your bird with fruits and vegetables to supplement its base diet of seeds and nuts. If your bird eats healthily, then there is no need to worry about any deficiency.

Chapter Seven: Caring for Your Bird's Health and Getting the Right Vet

Seizures

Some parrots suffer from mild to severe seizures that are characterized by twitching or convulsing. It can be a result of heavy metal poisoning, dehydration or other illnesses. If caused by heavy metal poisons, you will notice that your bird is lethargic, is vomiting, picking out its feathers, suffers from weight loss or has bloody or green droppings. You need to get immediate veterinary attention, otherwise, your bird's condition can get worse and it may suffer loss of motor function control or become disoriented or unconscious.

When your bird is dehydrated, there is a big chance that it can have seizures as well. However, after you rehydrate your bird and it still shows the same symptoms, it may have an underlying sickness that you should be concerned about like diabetes or a vitamin deficiency. Pox virus or aspergillosis can also bring about seizures. Don't disregard it, as it can prove fatal to your pet.

Chapter Seven: Caring for Your Bird's Health and Getting the Right Vet

Cancer

Birds are also prone to cancerous tumors, especially as they age. While they can develop lipomas or fatty tumors that are benign, it can only happen when the Amazon parrot is overweight. The bird can also develop a fibroma or tumor in the wing that may require its wing to be amputated. The usual substances that cause cancer in birds include viruses, pesticides, herbicides, radiation and second hand smoke.

Cloacal Papillomas

Some birds can have blood in their stool or they can have a hard time defecating. You can check if your bird has a reddish growth that is bulging from its vent. If this is the case, go to a vet immediately. And if you have other parrots in the cage, you need to separate the affected one as cloacal papillomas are transmissible.

Chapter Seven: Caring for Your Bird's Health and Getting the Right Vet

Getting the Right Parrot Doctor

Having an Amazon parrot for a pet is a lifelong commitment and entails a lot of responsibility. Not only do they require a lot of social interaction, they are high maintenance in the sense that you should always keep their homes and their accessories clean and well-maintained. You should also observe their behaviors closely to check for any signs of disorder whether physically or psychologically. It is also crucial that you get your Amazon parrot a checkup every yearly an avian veterinarian for any physical or behavioral problems.

Not all veterinarians are equal. Some are more trained in dealing with specific species of animals. Some vets can only treat cats and dogs. You need an avian veterinarian for your bird. These are animal doctors who are specially trained in the field of avian medicine. Ask reputable sources for a recommendation. How would you know if your vet is truly an avian vet? Here are some tips:

Chapter Seven: Caring for Your Bird's Health and Getting the Right Vet

- He knows what kind of bird you own. If the anima doctor cannot differentiate a cockatoo from a cockatiel, he may not be an avian vet.

- He is not afraid of holding or handling your bird. He cannot properly diagnose your bird if it is in the cage. A physical examination is a must, and he cannot just rely on your words.

- He weighs your bird. An accurate scale (gram) is needed to correctly calibrate the dose of medicine needed. A true avian vet does not just "feel the keel".

- He takes more than 15 minutes to check your bird. If the vet can easily diagnose your bird's condition in under 10 to 15 minutes, he may not really know what he is doing. A routine check-up is absolutely necessary and a good avian vet will advise you to have annual visits, even when there is no problem and especially if you have a young bird.

Chapter Seven: Caring for Your Bird's Health and Getting the Right Vet

When you call the animal hospital for a schedule, the receptionist may tell you that you cannot bring your bird out when it is too cold. Ask the avian vet. A true avian vet can give you plenty of good advice on how to keep your Amazon parrot warm as you bring it to the hospital, instead of letting you keep it at home without help.

Additionally, when you are in a true avian clinic, the support staff will be able to discuss all things related to the health of your bird, including proper diet. Most of the problems of Amazon parrots and other birds come from a bad diet or malnutrition so it is necessary that giving your bird the proper diet is discussed.

When choosing an avian veterinarian for your pet parrot check his qualifications. Find out how long he has been working with birds and the extent of his experience. Check to see if he has a lot of experience and Amazon parrots as patients. If his clinic takes emergencies and he can be available after hours, then he is a good choice. Visit his office or clinic before you bring your Amazon parrot. Seeing that it is clean and the staffs are friendly can be an influence

Chapter Seven: Caring for Your Bird's Health and Getting the Right Vet

in your decision. Also, the cost for a check-up is also a factor and checkups with avian vets are not cheap, so make sure that it is worth every penny you will pay.

Common Dangers inside the Home

Not only should you be wary of bacterial or viral infections and other illnesses, you should also be careful with certain household items as they can be the reason your bird can get sick or injured.

Ceiling fans

If you are bringing your bird out of the cage, make sure that ceiling fans are turned off. Better yet, try not to install ceiling fans when you have a bird at home so that you don't risk injuries. Don't even think that your bird won't be able to fly high enough to reach it. You would be surprised at what your bird can do.

Chapter Seven: Caring for Your Bird's Health and Getting the Right Vet

<u>Standing water</u>

Your bird can drown in water glasses, bath tubs, fish tanks, toilets, dog bowls or even in soaked dishes in your sink. Whenever you let your bird out of the cage, make sure that there is no standing water around.

- Scented candles or air fresheners. While it may smell good and you like it, the chemicals emitted by scented candles and air fresheners can be hazardous for your bird. Potpourri, scented teas and even boiling cinnamon sticks can have the same effects.

- Hot pots and pans. Do not let your bird out of the cage when you have pots or pans with hot or boiling food or water in it.

- Nonstick surfaces. Your cookware, popcorn maker or space heater can be made of non-stick surfaces and these can emit toxic fumes that are deadly to your pet parrot. Opt for stainless steel materials instead. Better yet, make sure that your home is well-ventilated.

Chapter Seven: Caring for Your Bird's Health and Getting the Right Vet

- Glass or mirror. A flying bird will not be able to distinguish when there is glass or a mirror in front of it and can crash on it and get injured or killed.

- Lead. Do you have fishing weights or stained glass in the house? Or anything that has chipped paint? This can contain lead and poison your Amazon parrot should it get near it and ingest it.

- Open windows and doors. Your pet Amazon parrot can fly away and you will never see it again. Or it can wander out into your yard and become easy prey for predators around the area.

- New carpets. When new carpets are installed, they emit deadly fumes that can kill your birds.

- Wires. Your pet parrot can chew on wires or become entangled and choked.

Chapter Seven: Caring for Your Bird's Health and Getting the Right Vet

Signs that Your Amazon Parrot May Be Sick or Injured

Your Amazon parrot may be suffering from an illness or injury and may need immediate professional attention when:

- Its demeanor has changed: a normally active bird will be lethargic when it is not feeling well
- It sleeps too much
- It crouches at the bottom of its cage
- It has discharge on its nostrils
- There is discharge at the base of its beak
- There are bubbles coming out of its beak
- There is clicking sound in its beak
- It bobs its tail
- It vomits
- It is unkempt and does not preen
- There is bleeding
- Its leg is hanging or a toe is ripped off
- It has an eye injury
- It has broken or bloody feathers

Chapter Seven: Caring for Your Bird's Health and Getting the Right Vet

- It becomes aggressive and dislikes touch, even though it is normally sweet

If you cannot bring your Amazon parrot to an avian vet immediately, you can prepare a "hospital cage" to house it in. It is a warm and safe pace that keeps your bird away from things that stress it. Here are instructions on how to prepare a hospital cage:

- Using paper towels, cover a 10-gallon fish tank
- In one end of the tank, put a rolled-up hand towel
- Put a heating pad on "low" heat and arrange it under one half of the tank (the other half should not be in the heating pad)
- Cover the top of the fish tank with a screen then use a towel to cover the hospital cage three-fourths of the way
- Put a shallow water dish. Don't put too much water, just less than an inch, or your bird might drown.

Chapter Seven: Caring for Your Bird's Health and Getting the Right Vet

- Place some of your Amazon parrot's favorite foods
- The hospital cage should be in a quiet place and the temperature should not be too warm. Allow your bird to rest and recuperate, but take it to the vet as soon as possible. The hospital cage is only temporary.

Chapter Seven: Caring for Your Bird's Health and Getting the Right Vet

Conclusion

The Amazon parrot is truly a delightful bird to have as a pet. After reading this book, you may have grown fond of this amazing bird and have the desire to get one and train it to be your companion for life. Well, that is not surprising. The Amazon parrot is indeed a magnificent, intelligent bird that is capable of surprising you with its unique talents and its magnetic charm.

Even though taking care of an Amazon parrot may require great effort, time and resources, you need to understand that your efforts will not be in vain. Keeping a pet of any kind will require commitment. It will entail great responsibility. But if you look at the rewards that come with having a pet by your side—it is all worth it. The joy and companionship you gain is something that will enrich your life, something that you will treasure forever.

Often, people in this day and age are bombarded with stress and they cannot create a work-life balance. Even children face stress on a daily basis because of the burdens of school work as well as peer pressure. But keeping a pet at home, especially a pet that can communicate with you, can bring such a relief from stress as well as create companionship that is good for people's mental health.

Having a pet that you can sound off to at the end of the day can be a pretty big deal. How about having a pet that can sing to you? That is even more amazing. Well, you can have that with a pet Amazon parrot. It may not be as playful as a dog that you can run with or play fetch with, but it can wrestle with you and climb on your shoulders. It can play tricks with you and even show off its dancing skills. An Amazon parrot is a pet that prefers socializing, so if you need a bit of relaxation and fun at the end of a tiring day, what better thing that to come home to a pet that will interact with you?

So don't be afraid to get a pet. Even more, don't be afraid to get a bird for a pet. Not as cuddly as a dog or cat, but just as curious and smart. It is both complex and delightful because Amazon parrots are sensitive and intelligent. People often joke that "forever" is not true, because people easily change their minds or their preferences that they cut off their relationships easily. But parrots are different—when they mate, they mate for life. When you bring a parrot home and it chooses you to be its person, then it is dedicated to you for life. That means, it will desire your attention and affection for life. As you care for it and spend time interacting with it, your bond will deepen. And since an Amazon parrot's lifespan is up to 60 years, you will have a companion for life.

Loyalty and love for a lifetime, how about that? Getting an Amazon parrot can be one of the best choices you will ever make!

Glossary of Important Terms

Addled eggs - These eggs are not viable and will not hatch.

Afterfeather - A structure that projects from the shaft of the feather at the rim of the superior umbilicus.

Allopreening - An act of social grooming amongst birds, in which one bird preens the other or a pair of birds does so mutually.

alternate plumage - The plumage of birds displayed in time for courtship or a breeding season.

Altricial - hatchlings with their eyes closed, and are not capable of leaving the nest on its own, and relies on parents for food.

Alula - a bird's "thumb"

Anisodactylus - a bird foot which has three toes pointing forward and one toe pointing at the back

Anting - a behaviour when birds rub insects, typically ants, on their feathers and skin

Aviculture - captive breeding and raising of birds

Back - exterior area of a bird's upper parts between its mantle and rump

basic plumage - non-breeding plumage

Beak - bill or rostrum

beak trimming - the partial removal of the beak

Belly - the area beneath the chest of a bird

Billing - a tendency of mated pairs that strengthen couple bonding

bird banding - a tag attached to the leg of a bird to enable identification

bird strike - bird/s that impact with planes in flight

Body down - soft, down feathers underneath a birds outer feathers.

Breast - body part between throat and belly

breeding plumage - plumage displayed by birds during breeding season

Brood - offspring birds

brood patch - an area of bare skin well supplied with blood vessels at the surface, and facilitates the transfer of heat to the eggs

Call - bird vocalization intending to serve as warning alarm

Cloaca - birds expel waste from it; other mate by joining cloaca; females lay eggs from this region

contact call - to make known to their kind the location of a bird

Crissum - feathered area between the vent and the tail

cryptic plumage - plumage meant to camouflage birds

definitive plumage - plumage completely developed and fixed

Down - the softest of the birds feathers

Egg - where birds develop until hatched

egg incubation - act of warming the eggs to promote hatching

Eye-ring - visible ring of feathers surrounding a bird's eyes

Feather - distinct outer "garment" covering a birds' body

feather pecking - a behavioural problem when one bird repeatedly pecks at the feathers of another bird

Fledge - a young bird that completely develops its wing muscles and feather suitable for flight

Fledgling - the period when a completely formed young bird ventures out of the nest and learns to take flight

Flight - the act of soaring in the air with the use of wings

Gizzard - specialized stomach organ found in the digestive tract of some birds used to grind up food and aided with grit or stone particles

Gleaning - a bird strategy used to catch insect prey

Grooming - the act of preening and self-cleaning

Iris - coloured outer ring surrounding birds' pupil

Lek - male aggression when in competition for the attention of a female

Mantle - front area of a bird's upper portion found between nape and top back

Migration - seasonal movement of birds

Morph - a polymorphic plumage colour variance between the same species

Moult - a periodic shedding and replacement of feathers

Nail - hard tissue at the tip of a bird's beak

Nares - two holes leading to the nasal cavities in the bird's skull

Nest - a bird's lair and home; where a female lays eggs and roosts

Over-brooding - a phenomenon when birds continue to brood eggs not likely to hatch

Passerine - any bird of the order Passeriformes

Pinioning - the removal of the joint of a bird's wing farthest from the body preventing flight

Plumage - refers to feathers covering a bird as well as pattern, colour and arrangement of feathers

Plumeology - the study of feathers

pre-alternate moult - also known as the prenuptial moult when basic plumage is shed to make way for nuptial plumage

prebasic moult - moult birds go through after breeding season

Precocial - young birds that after hatched has their eyes open

Preening - grooming od feathers in birds

Quill - the main stem of a feather where all structures branch from

Resident - a non-migratory bird

rictal bristles stiff, tapering feathers around the eyes of some birds

Rosette - a found at the corners of the beaks of some birds. A fleshy rosette area

Rump - area of a bird's body between the end of the back and the base of the tail

sexual dimorphism - common occurrence amongst birds in which males and females of a similar sort display different character traits

Song - bird vocalization associated with courtship

Speculum - A patch of typically bright coloured feathers, often iridescent

Sternum - bird's breastbone

Syrinx - the vocal organs of birds

Tail streamers - narrow tips of the tail of some birds

Talon - claw of bird of prey

Teleoptiles - feathers of an adult bird

Throat - body area located between the chin and the upper part of the breast

Thigh - body part between knee and trunk of the bird's body

Vent - the outer opening of the cloaca

Wings - The bird's forelimbs that are the essential to flight

Wingspan - distance between wings from one wing tip to the other

Photo Credits

Page Photo by user Animal People Forum via Flickr.com,

https://www.flickr.com/photos/animalpeopleforum/23767376899/

Page Photo by user Erick Houli via Flickr.com,

https://www.flickr.com/photos/bejor77/16223888879/

Page Photo by user Gregory "Slobirdr" Smith via Flickr.com,

https://www.flickr.com/photos/slobirdr/12792959235/

Page Photo by user Kurt Bauschardt via Flickr.com,

https://www.flickr.com/photos/kurt-b/11846299473/

Page Photo by user Petr Kosina via Flickr.com,

https://www.flickr.com/photos/clobrda/5899685524/

Page Photo by user Nathan Rupert via Flickr.com,

https://www.flickr.com/photos/nathaninsandiego/6254217374/

Page Photo by user Josh More via Flickr.com,

https://www.flickr.com/photos/guppiecat/34764492333/

Page Photo by user Geek2Nurse via Flickr.com,

https://www.flickr.com/photos/ladylong/78209284/

Page Photo by user Nathan Rupert via Flickr.com, https://www.flickr.com/photos/nathaninsandiego/8001432427/

Page Photo by user Charles Patrick Ewing via Flickr.com, https://www.flickr.com/photos/132033298@N04/21842483383/

References

Amazon Parrot – Lafeber.com

https://lafeber.com/pet-birds/species/amazon-parrot/

Amazon Parrot Care Sheet – AvianAndExotic.com

http://www.avianandexotic.com/care-sheets/birds/amazon-parrot/

5 Things You Need to Know About Amazon Parrots – Petcha.com

http://www.petcha.com/5-things-you-need-to-know-about-amazon-parrots/

Facts about Amazon – The Spruce Pets

https://www.thesprucepets.com/facts-about-amazon-parrots-390263

Amazon Parrots Grooming – PurrsNGrrs.com

http://purrsngrrs.com/amazon-parrots-grooming/

Common Diseases of Amazon Parrot – TheNest.com

https://pets.thenest.com/common-diseases-amazon-parrot-10472.html

Amazon Parrot - Drsfostersmith.com

https://www.drsfostersmith.com/pic/article.cfm?aid=1929

Amazon Parrots from South America – BeautyofBirds.com

https://www.beautyofbirds.com/amazons.htm

Owning an Amazon Parrot as a Pet – Mom.me

https://animals.mom.me/owning-amazon-parrot-pet-4874.html

Amazon Parrots – Feeding – VCAHospitals.com

https://vcahospitals.com/know-your-pet/amazon-parrots-feeding

Basics of Parrot Taming and Training – TrainedParrot.com

http://trainedparrot.com/Taming/

www.ingramcontent.com/pod-product-compliance
Lightning Source LLC
Chambersburg PA
CBHW060838050426
42453CB00008B/739